Gopher's Loafers

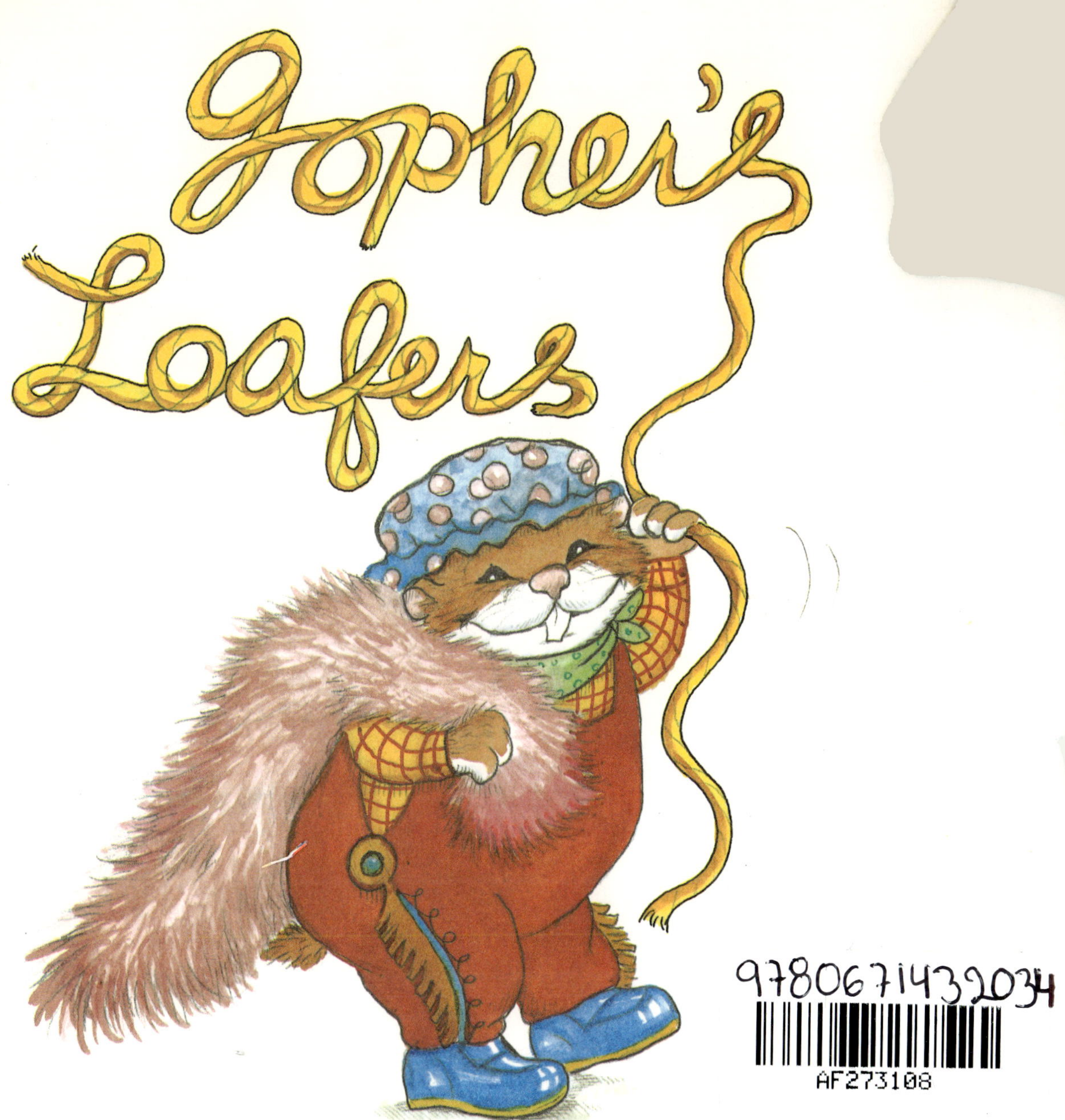

by H. L. Ross
Illustrated by Amye Rosenberg

LITTLE SIMON
Published by Simon & Schuster, New York

All summer long, Goldie tried to learn how to tie
her sneakers. She watched how the grown-ups did
it and tried to do the same, but all she wound up
with was a big mess of string.

She was sick and tired of asking other people to tie her shoes for her. So, she buried her sneakers in the backyard and went out to buy herself a pair of loafers.

No one in the first grade class was surprised
when Goldie came in on the first day of school
wearing loafers.

Now, everyone knows that gophers simply do
not wear loafers!

Gophers wear high-topped sneakers. The sneakers are usually black, but sometimes they are other colors.

But they all remembered how, last year in
kindergarten, Goldie came to school one day
wearing a feathered boa

and on another day wearing a big hat with flowers.

And once she even wore a shower cap and a cowgirl outfit!

It was true, Goldie liked to be different.

So, when Goldie came to school wearing loafers instead of traditional gopher high tops, no one paid any attention to her.

No one, that is, except the teacher, who paid
plenty of attention to her.

"Goldie, my girl," said the teacher. "I see you are
wearing loafers today. That is certainly unusual,
and fine for today, I suppose. But tomorrow, you
must wear your high-topped sneakers. Ms. Gulch,
the principal, is coming to our classroom to see
how nicely each and every one of you has learned
to tie his or her own shoes over the summer."

Goldie was a very worried gopher when she went home that afternoon.

She even tried to dig up her sneakers. But the dog had already found them.

The next day, Ms. Gulch, came to the classroom. Everyone watched while Grant Gopher tied his sneakers, as neat as a pin. Everyone watched while Greta Gopher tied a fancy double knot in hers. And they oohed and aahed as the twins, Gilly and Golly, tied each other's laces at the same time.

When it was Goldie's turn to tie her laces, Ms. Gulch said: "Loafers on a gopher? Well, I never! I guess I'll have to make a special trip through here next Monday just to watch Goldie tie a pair of proper gopher high-topped-sneaker laces."

Goldie went home that afternoon feeling more worried than ever. At dinner, she scarcely touched her tumbleweed tetrazini and ate only a bit of her nutcracker sweets.

After dinner, she sat out on the porch and stared
at the prairie stars and wished she were someplace
where there was no such thing as shoelaces.

"What's all of this sighing about?" said Grandpa
Captain Gopher, who had just that very day
returned home from the sea.
  "We were supposed to learn how to tie our high-
topped sneakers over the summer," said Goldie.
"But I just couldn't get the hang of it."

"I don't see why you can't," said Grandpa. "You never know when you might get tired of wearing those loafers."

"But what can I do?" Goldie asked.

"Come here, and I'll tell you a little story."

Grandpa took out a small stick and wound a rope around it. "Pretend this stick is your sneaker and this rope is your shoelace.

This string is Fox and the other is Hare.

Well, Fox and Hare were chasing each other around.

Fox ran up a tree.

Hare ran around it once and climbed through a hole in the trunk to the other side."

And with that, Grandpa had tied a bow.

"Let me try that!" said Goldie.
Goldie told the story to Grandpa and, when she
had finished, she had tied a bow, too.

Every night that week after dinner, Goldie sat
out on the porch with Grandpa, holding the stick
and rope, and telling the story of Fox and Hare.
And each time she finished, she'd tied a bow.

The next Monday, true to her word, Ms. Gulch came to the classroom just to watch Goldie tie her shoes. To her distress, Goldie still wore loafers.

"I don't have any high-tops, Ms. Gulch, but I'd be happy to tie yours," said Goldie.

And before Ms. Gulch could say a word, Goldie had untied and tied both of Ms. Gulch's sneakers.

And so, Goldie continued to wear loafers. And one day or so out of every month, she'd wear a pair of high-topped sneakers just like all the other gophers wore so that she could stay in practice tying a bow.

Maybe one day she would wear high-topped sneakers every day, but then again, maybe she wouldn't. After all, a gopher with loafers is a very unusual sight. "And what's wrong with being unusual?" said Goldie.

Take scissors and cut out Goldie Gopher's clothing. Remember, don't cut too close to the staples that hold Goldie's book together!

Slit here—carefully slip over head
SHERIFF

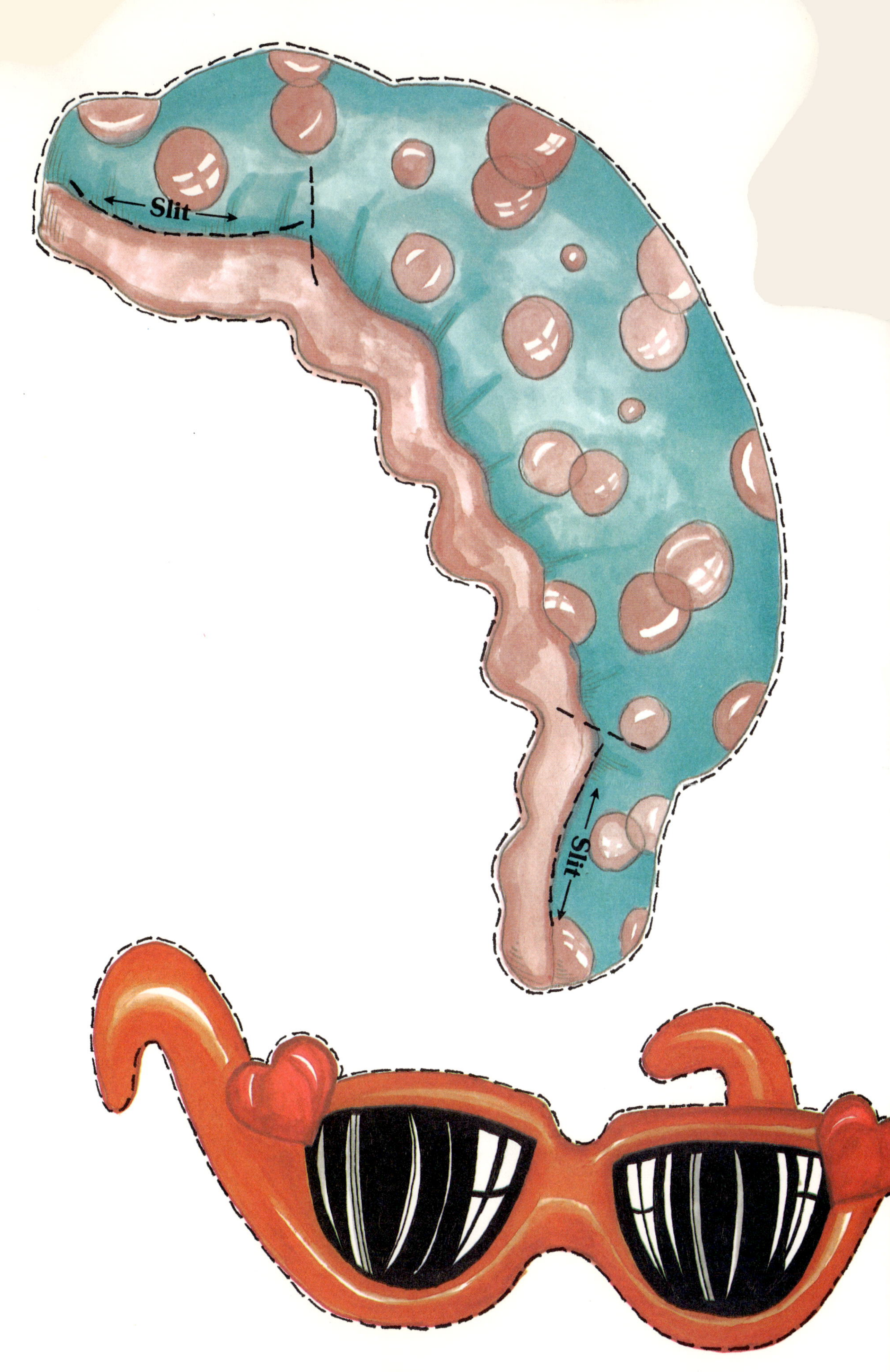
Slit
Slit

Cut out skirt
Cut on dotted line below all the way to the end
Cut slit
Fold and insert tab into slit
← Cut →
← Cut on line →
Slit
Fold
Fold here

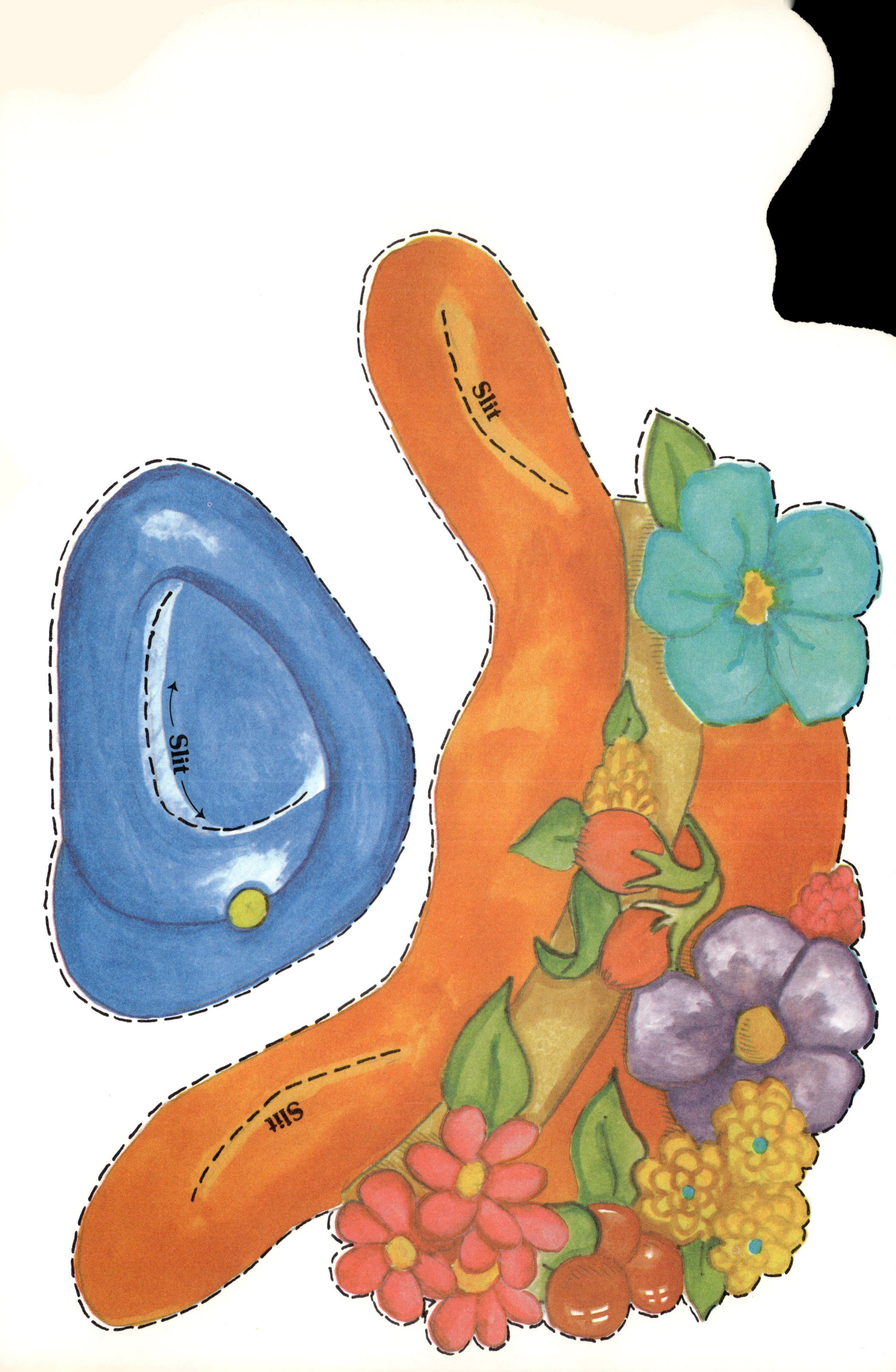

Slit
Slit
Slit